Terry Treetop Saves The Dolphin

Tali Carmi

Terry Treetop
Saves The Dolphin

Written by Tali Carmi

Terry Treetop Saves The Dolphin\Tali Carmi

Copyright © 2014 by Tali Carmi

All rights reserved. No part of this book may be used or reproduced in any manner whatsoever without the written and signed permission of the author, except in the case of brief quotations embodied in critical articles or review

First edition - 10/2014

ISBN: 978-965-92331-7-5

Contact information: tbcarmi@gmail.com

Author website: www.thekidsbooks.com

Twitter: @tbcarmi

This book is dedicated to my beloved parents

Uri and Bracha Perry

for their 80th birthday

On this summer vacation, Terry went camping with his parents to a marine nature reserve.

On the first day, he was so excited that he awoke extra early and sought out the highest tree to climb. After all, everybody did call him "Terry Treetop" because he loved climbing trees.

He wanted to discover the lay of the land, and that could only be done from up high.

Terry used his binoculars to look around. In all directions he could see varying shades of blue.

Not far from the beach, he saw something popping up out of the water then splashing back in. It was a group of dolphins jumping, playing, and making noises together. It was as if they were competing to see who the highest jumper was.

A small dolphin was swimming near his mother. He jumped as high as he could, but he was still a baby and could not jump that high. Terry laughed at his water tricks and decided to name him Dido.

His mother was watching and teaching him the ways of the sea.

Terry realized that baby dolphins are just like kids who try to act grown up.

Terry wanted to be friends with Dido and play with him.

He quickly climbed down the tree and ran to the deck where he stood and waved to the dolphins.

"Hey!" Terry shouted. "Come closer and play with me." He jumped up and down to grab the dolphins' attention, and when they finally noticed him, they were just as curious about Terry as he was of them.

The grown-ups were hesitant, and slowly swam far away from the beach. But Dido was focused on Terry and quickly started to swim towards him.

He wanted to have a closer look at this strange creature that was standing outside of the water on two legs. He had never seen anything like it before.

As Dido came closer to the deck, he did not notice a fisherman's net that was left in the water. He continued swimming and went right through a hole in the net.

His mother hurried after him, but the hole was much too small for her to swim through.

She was distressed because she was unable to help him.

When Dido noticed that he was caught in the net, he whistled to his mother for help, but she could not help him.

"Oh no," said Terry, "that net was not supposed to be here, and now you're caught in it." Dido whistled back sadly.

Terry was a good swimmer in his home swimming pool, but here it was the sea with no lifeguards around.

"Don't worry! I'm going to get help; I will not abandon you."

Terry looked around. It was still early morning and there was no one on the beach. He used his binoculars to survey all around him, but he did not see anybody that could help him.

Then he had an idea. He would climb a tree to get a better view.

Terry climbed high and peered through the binoculars. Now he could see a ranger's boat.

Terry waved and called to him, but the boat was so far away that he could not hear him.

So, Terry had another idea. Many birds were sitting on the higher branches of the tree. Terry shook the tree and all of the birds flew up and cawed to the sky and the sea.

Luckily, the flock of birds drew the attention of the ranger, and he saw Terry waving from the tree.

He knew that the little boy was trying to tell him something, so he waved back to him and turned his boat towards the deck.

Terry knew that he understood, so he climbed down the tree to meet the ranger.

When the ranger came closer, he saw the dolphin caught in the net. "Hey ranger," Terry said, "I'm Terry, please help this little dolphin!"

"Hi Terry. I'm Roger, the marine nature reserve ranger. This is so sad; fishermen leave their nets behind and dolphins get caught in them. But don't worry, I will help him."

The ranger put on his mask, air tank, and diving wetsuit. He grabbed his cutter to cut the net with, and jumped into the water, swimming right over to Dido.

He cautiously cut away the net, being careful not to hurt the dolphin.

Dido was no longer afraid because he understood that this man was there to help.

After he was freed, Dido swam directly to his mother. He was very tired and weak, but his mother was now beside him.

She swam under him and helped him surface the water to breathe.

Terry noticed that dolphins breathe air just like people, but as marine mammals, they can stay under water for long periods of time.

Terry watched as the dolphins flocked together. They were jumping and making happy noises just as before.

He was happy for them, but sad too. "Why are you sad?" the ranger asked him.

"Thank you for the help, I am happy that the dolphin was saved, but I am sad that I don't get to play with him," Terry said.

Terry reminded Roger of himself as a little boy. He had wanted to play with dolphins too.

He had an idea. "You can still play with the dolphin, let me show you," he said. Roger handed him a lifejacket, mask, and a lifebuoy. "Wear this!" he said to Terry as he helped him into the mask.

Roger grabbed a ball and they both jumped into the water.

Roger threw the ball towards Dido, and the little dolphin immediately understood the game. He used his nose to bounce the ball back to him.

"You are so smart!" Terry said, laughing with glee. "Now, we can really play together."

Dido whistled at Terry, as if he were laughing right along with him.

"Terry, you are a hero," said Roger. "Will you be my helper for the week?" "Yes," Terry replied with great joy.

He decided that he will be a ranger when he grows up so he can help animals in need and teach people how to keep the environment safe.

"This vacation is going to be really special!" he said with a smile.

Thank You!

This book has been created with love and joy
And it is very important for me to hear
what you think about it.
Please press the link below and leave a review.
Your thoughts mean a lot to me.

Lot's of Love
- Tali

My dear readers:

Thank you for purchasing *Terry Treetop Saves The Dolphin*, the fourth book of my Adventure & Education Children's Books series.

I really enjoyed writing about this little boy and his adventure at the marine nature reserve, and I hope you too enjoyed it.

I appreciate that you chose to buy and read my book over some of the others out there. Thank you for putting your confidence in me to help educate and entertain your kids.

If you and your children enjoyed *Terry Treetop Saves The Dolphin* and you have a couple of spare minutes now, it would really help me out if you would like to leave me a review (even if it's short) on Amazon. All these reviews really help me spread the word about my books and encourage me to write more and add more to the series! Click here to leave a review. If you'd like to read another one of my children's books, I've included more information on the next page for you.

Sincerely yours,

Tali Carmi

Books by Tali Carmi

 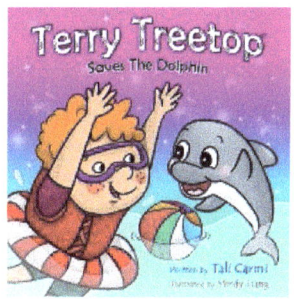 

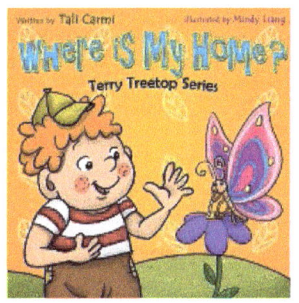 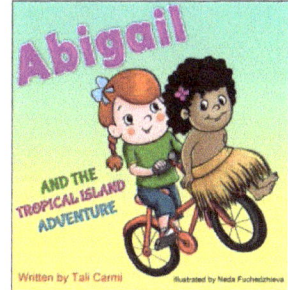 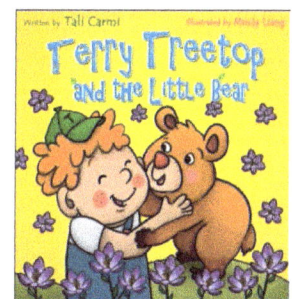

www.ingramcontent.com/pod-product-compliance
Lightning Source LLC
Chambersburg PA
CBHW061349010526
44107CB00011B/878